Seduced

*A spine-tingling, toe-curling collection of poetry and prose
that leave you wanting more.*

r. A. bentinck

FYAPUBLISHING | GEORGETOWN

Seduced

Copyright © 2018 by **r. A. bentinck**

All rights reserved. No part of this publication may be reproduced, distributed or transmitted in any form or by any means, without prior written permission.

FyaPublishing
95 South Turkeyen,
Georgetown, Guyana.

Seduced/ **r. A. bentinck**
ISBN **978-0999444535**

Cover design by r.A. bentinck
Cover image by ractapopulous

All great lovers are articulate, and verbal seduction is the surest road to actual seduction. - *Marya Mannes*

Seduced

r. A. bentinck

Contents

Author's Preface 11

The Breakfast Table 13

Fine Wine 15

Hypnotic Eyes 16

Intoxicated 17

Just One Thought 18

Kissing King 19

Lazy Days 20

Like Fine Wine 21

Linger a Little Longer 22

Morning Wish 24

Romancing the Wine 25

Flaming Desires 26

Smile 27

Smooth Jazz and Fine Wine 29

Sunday Mornings 31

The Aftermath 32

Seduced

The Little Things	33
The Moon Smiles	35
This World of Mine	36
Time	37
We Make Music	38
Whispering Flowers	40
Pillows and Sheets	41
The Sweetness from Your Lips.	42
Naked	43
Cooling Relief	45
Expectations	46
Making it Hard	48
Curves	50
Breezy Relief	51
Desirable	52
In Your Eyes	53
Light Your Fire	54
Signature Sounds	55
Soaked	57

The Shower 58

Unlocked 59

Against the Wall 60

Late Night Dinner 61

Her Pink Lingerie 62

Feline Tendencies 64

I Wanna 66

I Wish 67

Impatient 68

In My Mind 70

Peaceful Sleep 71

Pulsating Petals 72

Salty Nectar 73

She Said… 74

Slow and Easy 75

Suddenly 77

Fantasies 79

What You Gonna Do? 80

Whatever 81

Seduced

Misinterpretation	83
Don't Speak	84
Your Embrace	85
One More Time	86
Just to Please	87
The Teasing Game	88
Unfulfilled Desires	89
All Yours	90
Finally	91
Those Moments	93
Led	95
Roaming Tongue	97
She is Unbelievable	99
In the Rain	100
The Artist at Work	102
Undressing	104
Turning Petals	106
Rhythms	107
Waiting	108

Unfinished 109

Poetess 110

Satisfaction 111

In the Dark 112

Glistening 113

Chasing Flavours 114

Doing Dishes 115

Her 116

One 117

Picking Fruits 118

Secrets 119

Tell Me 121

You're 122

The Proclamation 123

Instigating 124

Let Me 125

Dangerous 126

Midnight 127

My Plea 128

Seduced

Touched 130

Transgressing Eyes 131

In this Moment 132

Tonight 133

Of all the Things 134

Velvet Screams 135

One Dance (Gingerbay Café) 136

Falling Clothes 139

Don't Make Me Wait 140

Fatal Whispers 141

Her Skirt 142

Scented Trail 143

The Wild Side 144

Dirty Desires 146

Steamy 148

Unchained Desires 149

Risqué Roulette 150

Pillow Fight 151

On the Phone 153

Waking Me Up 154

I Love 155

On Those Days 157

Magical Fingers 158

Speechless 159

Lavish Longings 160

Morning Ride 161

Shower Exist 162

Come Back Baby 163

Dreams 165

Take Back 166

Show Me the Way 167

Rainy Days 168

Whispers 169

Give Me a Reason 171

All Over Me 172

Underneath the Sheets 173

Drizzled Honey 175

Reflection 177

Seduced

Fooling Around - Scene 1 178

Fooling Around - Scene 2 180

Fooling Around - Scene 3 182

P.M. Scenes 183

Slow Surrender 185

Unbuttoning 186

Pretty Feet 187

Lustful Longing 188

Don't Stop 189

Penetration 190

Let's Do It Again 191

Sleepless 193

Nightly Pleasures 194

I Need More 195

The Spot 197

The Text Message 198

Scream My Name 199

Flavours 200

Intimidation 201

- Burn Baby 202
- Exploration 204
- Catch the Fire 205
- Gradually 206
- I Can't Explain 207
- The Phone Call 208
- The Taste of You 209
- Thirst 210
- Forbidden 211
- The Kitchen Counter 212
- Climaxing 214
- About The Author 215

Seduced

r. A. bentinck

Author's Preface

The modern art of seduction is knowing what someone desires and willingly fulfilling those nefarious desires. You find a way to seduce them to the point where you not only take their breath away but also leave them with a spine-tingling, toe-curling sensation long after the glorious deed is done.

This intriguing poetry collection brings together an extensive variety of modern poetry and evocative prose which exemplify the extraordinary power and sensuous beauty of seduction.

From the celebration of those awe-inspiring moments with that specific person as is clear in **Kissing King** to those more heart-pounding moments of coitus that **Feline Tendencies** enshrines.

Let's face it, seduction and being seduced will continue to be an integral part of our lives. So, celebrate it. Learn about it. Master the art of seducing and be free-spirited enough to indulge in it without any inhibitions.

Georgetown,

February 2021

Seduced

r. A. bentinck

The Breakfast Table

this breakfast table is
reserved for dining only!

it's always
meticulously designed
to please
and
to satisfy
the eating experience.

but today,
we break all
the dining rules.

plates get tossed!
drinking glasses
get knocked over,
chairs get shoved aside,
the tablecloth gets
extremely wrinkled.

Seduced

the table is shifting
in countless directions
and
this once neat
and
organised surface
has become a battleground
for
bare-naked bodies
moving
with the flow of
lust filled rhythms.

r. A. bentinck

Fine Wine

you are like aged
fine wine.

you should be
slowly sipped
and savoured
from expensive crystal
by appreciating
and
deserved lips.

never gulped
by hungry and
unappreciative mouth.
your every
flavour
must be
savoured
by all the taste buds.

Seduced

Hypnotic Eyes

i lose my way
in your tender gaze
as your eyes
wrestle mine.

i get consumed
in the eternity
of your stare.

your eyes tell
a thousand tales
of tenderness,
love, lust, longing,
and
insatiable desires.
i get hypnotised
by your sedating eyes
and lost in the eternity
of your gaze.

r. A. bentinck

Intoxicated

i can taste the
salacious words
at the tips
of your succulent lips
and
i get intoxicated.

i embraced
your glistening body
and
your warm
slippery sweetness
make me drunk.

i can smell
the pure essence
of your natural fragrance
and
it makes me high.

Just One Thought

just the thought
of you
and the days seem
brighter.

just a fleeting thought
of you
and old familiar
music
seems refreshingly new.

just one thought
of you
changes everything.

r. A. bentinck

Kissing King

she draws me in with
lips that's
tender and succulent,
she keeps me glued
with the slow
flow of her
honey flavours.

her kissing is celestial.

with every smack
of her lips
with every gentle kiss
she keeps me
wanting more
and more and more.
she has
transformed me
into a kissing king.

Seduced

Lazy Days

we lazed like
exhausted animals
on the first days
of summer.

we laugh
at time
as it wanders by.

we stuffed
the cares of
the week in
the back of
our minds
while we laze
the day away.

r. A. bentinck

Like Fine Wine

after all this time

you have matured

like fine wine-

bottled goodness,

priceless,

elegant,

ageless,

with a love

that's savoury.

Seduced

Linger a Little Longer

on days like this
when you look
so fine,
am tempted to ask…
please,
linger a little longer.

you light up
the atmosphere
with glorious vibes
and
electrifying smile,
why wouldn't you
linger a little longer?

i can't face the thought that
you must go so soon,
so i'm building up the courage
to say, please,
linger a little longer.

r. A. bentinck

it's not every day i get to
see you this way,
you ought to
linger a little longer.

i'm running out of reasons
to ask you to wait a while
so please,
just linger a little longer.

Seduced

Morning Wish

may your day
be as bright as
your sunrise smile.

your moments
as excited as
your eyes
when you the recall
pulsating moments
we shared.

this is my
morning wish
for you.

r. A. bentinck

Romancing the Wine

she moistened
the tips of her
rose pink lips and slowly closed
her eyes.
the words poured
from the depths
of her angelic soul.

with every word
she was brewing up
chilled heaven,
a wine frenzy.
she recollected
the memories
of soothing escapades.
without sipping
on a glass she made me
crave the opportunity,
to sit and dine with her wine.
she is a wine connoisseur.

Flaming Desires

i want to

seduce you

to the edge of

your

flaming desires

where

heart-pounding sensations

steal

your breath away.

r. A. bentinck

Smile

i see your face
with that
happy glow
and
i can't help
but greet you
with a smile.

i embrace you
with a flood
of affection
and electricity
ignite
our embrace
and
i can't help
but
smile.
you whisper
sweet softness

Seduced

in the halls of
my ear
the kind of words
that leaves me
helpless with
a smile.

in your presence
you give me
unlimited reasons
to do nothing
but
smile.

r. A. bentinck

Smooth Jazz and Fine Wine

a skilfully played
tenor saxophone
lured
your heightened senses
and
speak to you in
sultry tones
that's only
understood by
a thirsty soul.

unspeakable bliss
slowly coerce
you
to sip some more
of the liquid delight
and
you tamely surrender
to the subtleties of
your chilled seducer.

Seduced

the liquid lure

gently approaches

anxious lips

while

dim lights

take you

on a celestial journey

where the cares

of the day

just drift

like smoke in

gentle evening breeze.

r. A. bentinck

Sunday Mornings

the ease of the
morning breeze
greet us and gently fondle
our wayward desires.

the whistling birds
provide just enough
music to fertilise
the burgeoning emotions
that's germinating
in our overactive loins.

Sunday mornings
bring fresh flowers,
renewed excitement,
keys to release
imprisoned longings,
and unexpected
heart-pounding
discoveries.

The Aftermath

pitch-black stillness
in a cosy bedroom.

the moon
sneak a peak
through the crease
in the heavy curtain.

its beamy eyes
show the glistening
glow of your satisfied body
which
lay listless
in the aftermath
of a battle with
racy emotions.

r. A. bentinck

The Little Things

it's the little things
i wanna do with you.

i wanna run
and bathe
in the rain
with you.

i wanna stay
up all night
with you.

i wanna cook
nutritious meals
for you.

it's the little things
i wanna do for you.
i wanna hand-picked
roses

Seduced

for you.
i wanna play
the fool
for you.

i wanna be
there for you.

i wanna do
all these little things
just for you.

r. A. bentinck

The Moon Smiles

tonight,
the moon smiles generously
just because of you.

the sea breeze
whispers tranquilising
words of comfort
and we snuggle.

your company
lights up the dim environment
like a thousand fireflies.

tonight,
the moon smiles
just to reveal
another dimension
of your loveliness,
another dimension
of your lovingness.

Seduced

This World of Mine

i close

my eyes

and

in this world

of mine

you

fill it

with unspeakable

fondness.

r. A. bentinck

Time

i lay
in your arms
for a minute
and
i get lost in
the moment.

i open my eyes
and
the hours flashed by
during our moments of
sweetness.

time has no respect
for me
whenever i'm with you.

We Make Music

every time

our hearts meet

there is

a familiar rhythm

that

beats deep within

and

we get lost

in the dance of

enticing emotions.

it's just one

of the ways

we make music

we create

our own music

with body

heart and soul.

every time

r. A. bentinck

our hearts meet
there is
a familiar rhythm
that
beats deep within
and
we get lost
in the dance of
engaging emotions.

it's just one
of the many ways
we make music.

Whispering Flowers

flowers whisper
a quieting
and
inviting lullaby
to the honey bees…

come,
drink of my unending
fondness.
come,
taste my
fluid essence.

r. A. bentinck

Pillows and Sheets

with a coy smile
plastered on her face
she declared,
you leave but your scent
lingers on my pillows and sheets.

i relive every moment,
every emotion,
every sound,
like it's the real thing.

i know this might
sound eccentric,
but when you leave
i can still feel you,
see you, hear you, taste you,
just from smelling
the enchanting fragrance
you leave on my pillows and sheets.

The Sweetness from Your Lips.

i saw your lips
for the first times
and started
salivating over
it's perceived
sweetness
softness
succulence
and sumptuousness.

the first time we kissed
i tried to kiss
the honey from your lips
and got addicted.
today, i'm a happy lip addict
who has no problem
getting his daily fix
of kissing sweetness
from your lips.

Naked

on those rare
and
spontaneous occasions
when the carefree spirit
possess her,
she loves to amble
around the house
naked.

her every step
leaves
a crumb trail of
temptation
along the way.

she unconsciously toys
with my self-control switch.
her mindless saunters
trigger a spark of passion
that erupts beneath

Seduced

my calm and
composed demeanour.
a battle between
my senses ensue
each one fighting for
a position of dominance,
each
a victim of
her naked sex appeal.

Cooling Relief

after prolonged exposure
to the
searing heat
of excitement,
we sought
cooling relief
by the only
available window.

fiery bodies
welcomed the
soft kisses
from
the cooling breeze
oh,
what a sweet relief.

Seduced

Expectations

her relaxed body is
accompanied by
an anticipatory heartbeat.

her imagination takes
eagle's flight as
she waits.

expensive pearls
kiss her
priceless skin
that glistens in
the soft red light.

Victoria's secret
restrain the stirrings
in her overheating loins.
she is simmering.
she is ravished
by

r. A. bentinck

delectable thoughts
and
overcome by
the persistent
sensual anxiety.

she is trapped in
the arms of impending
carnal cravings.

Making it Hard

i know
you can see it.

i can definitely
feel it!

with that
penetrating stare
from across the room,
you're making it
hard on me!

your electrifying smile
leave me helpless.

i am trying, but
i can't fight it,
you're making it
hard for me.
i am thinking of

r. A. bentinck

all the things
i can do
to you,
all the things
i can do
with you.
you're making it
harder for me.

i know,
you know
i am excited.
i'm trying hard
but
i can't fight it.

everything about you
make me
want you
so badly.
you're making it
hard for me.

Curves

dainty curves
dominate the space
of the scented room.

every visual inch
of her elegant body
lures my parched
fleshly appetite.

her inviting smile
plead with my wild side
and
her innocent eyes
petition my carnal
desires to rise.

r. A. bentinck

Breezy Relief

simmering
in the afterglow
of erogenous passion.

we begged for cooling relief
in the absence
of a fan.

with opened windows
and
drawn curtains
we await the
lulling relief
of the
unpredictable wind.
we offer our bodies
to the mercies
of the sudden gush of
the refreshing breeze.

Desirable

her silky voice
caress my auditory faculties
and
send shivers
through my senses.

her bright
and
inviting eyes
call out to my soul
bringing a fond smile
to my face.

heavenly scents
whisk me off to
a celestial place
where
she satisfies
my every fantasy.

r. A. bentinck

In Your Eyes

that quiet look
in your eyes,
the one that
whips up storms
on the inside
sending my imagination
crazy.

that piercing look
in your eyes
that sends quivers
through my sensual faculties
leaving me with
uncontrollable urges.

that baby look in your eyes,
the one that say more than
words allow
with it, i can sense
your unconditional love.

Seduced

Light Your Fire

i am always enthralled
by the thought of
enkindling your fire.

with just one touch
your eyes begin
to glow,
your breasts get perky with delight,
and your lips
widen with expectations.

there is a fire
within you that
i love to ignite
just because it
heightens all
your senses
and allow your desires
to burn
brightly.

r. A. bentinck

Signature Sounds

by now
my ears are
finely tuned
to those
familiar sounds.

those
prolong moans
confirm that i've
hit those erogenous zones.

those
satisfying groans
that speaks of
the bittersweet pain
you crave
again and again.

those
pillow muffling screams

Seduced

that speaks
of your sweet release.
i'm always attentive
to your signature sounds
they speak of
your full contentment.

r. A. bentinck

Soaked

we are lost in
the deluge of feverish frenzy.

our possessed bodies
become generators
of unimaginable heat.

a room starved of fresh air,
the uncooperative breeze,
coupled with an insatiable yearning
trigger an overflow in
our perspiration glands.

now we are tussling in liquid excess.
slippery bodies
glisten from excitement.
loud panting dominates
the ear waves
and we toss like drifting wood
in rushing waters.

The Shower

our overheated bodies
smiled at the tranquillising effects
of the cooling
crystal drizzle from above.

water droplets
caress every inch
of her natural blessings
while desiring eyes gazed
in amazement,
inextinguishable desires
fleetly rises to the surface
once again,
suddenly,
clashing bodies cause
shower water
to splish-splash
all over the place
creating music with
a mouth-enticing rhythm.

r. A. bentinck

Unlocked

she sneaked
into the secret corners
of my heart
and unlocked
my hidden fantasies.

she nurtures
my wild sides
and impregnate
the freak in me.

these days,
my fantasies frolic
with unbridled freeness,
and my imagination gets
tested consistently.
since she unlocked
my hidden fancies,
life is more
excitingly carefree.

Against the Wall

pinned
against the wall
with limited space
to savour
her diverse flavours.

backed up against the wall
with no room
to groove and glide.

i'm relishing
the essence of your
maneuverability.

up against the wall
with little room
to play
we surrender to the power
of the moment.

r. A. bentinck

Late Night Dinner

with steamy lingerie
like that
let's do late night dinner
under the stars,

where the still of the night
sets the stage for
the soothing music of
the whispering wind.

i would love to have
the pleasure of dining with your smile
and enjoy the glow
of your excited eyes.
with erotic lingerie,
like this
let's make plans
for a late-night dinner
under the watchful eyes
of winking stars.

Her Pink Lingerie

erotic…
the first thought
that raced across
the halls of
my now
aroused mind.
she painted
a stunning portrait
in
her pink lingerie.

sultry…
was the image
she sculpted
posing in those
sexy pink lingerie.
irresistible…
was the smile
she flashed,
creating an

r. A. bentinck

elegant snapshot
in
her pink lingerie.

seductive…
the fragrance
she wore
that lit up
the atmosphere
complementing
her spine-tingling
pink lingerie.

Seduced

Feline Tendencies

every time the
pressures
of
pleasure
gets
too much to handle
she develops
feline tendencies.

scratching
and
clawing,
making strange
and
indistinguishable sounds.

whenever
the pressures
of
rapture

r. A. bentinck

get
too much to take,
anything and everything
is a fair game.

walls scream
from her clawing,
sheets wrinkle
under her
vice-like grip
while feeling
the wrath of her nails.

when
the pressures
of delight
get
too much
for her to negotiate
she develops lots of
uncontrollable
feline tendencies.

Seduced

I Wanna

i wanna ride you to the precipice
of your fluid imagination
where no rules exist.

i wanna flirt with your obscene obsessions
playing your dangerous
love games.

i wanna wrestle with your unending urges
just so you can
pin me into breathless submission.
i wanna bend you like a bow
just to accommodate
my anxious arrow.
i wanna travel with you to those
forbidden places
where we can live
dangerously
and our hearts beat
uncontrollably.

r. A. bentinck

I Wish

i wish
i could extend
the hands of time.

i wish
i could recoup
those wasted years.

i will
do whatever it takes
to prolong
these moments
in
your presence.

Impatient

hurry!
let's strip these
clothes off.
this changing process is taking
too long.

let's slip things
to the side
so we can appease
these dominating desires.

my craving for you
races ahead
of the undressing process.

let's skip
the prolong
foreplay formalities
and give in to these
overpowering overtures.

r. A. bentinck

let's forget
the comfort of the bed
and take the cold floor.

hurry!
let's disrobe
in a haste.

In My Mind

in my mind
i can taste the essence
of your invitational lips.

in my mind
i can feel the warmth
of your enticing embrace
which quenches my insatiable thirst.

in my mind
i can feel
electrifying sensations
seeping through my bone
making me excited.
in my mind
i can do all the things
i want to do
to you
just because its
in my mind.

r. A. bentinck

Peaceful Sleep

cradled

in the warmth

of her nakedness.

i drift away

in the bosom of

peaceful sleep.

her comforting caress

shield me from

the cold

and

unfriendly breeze

while i drift away

in a peaceful sleep.

Pulsating Petals

touched
with tantalising care.

seasoned
to sensual satisfaction.

fondled into a fit of frenzy.

toyed
into heightened tensions.

i have given
her flower full attention,
now her petals are
pulsating with gladness.

r. A. bentinck

Salty Nectar

in the heat
of the moment
i crave your tenderness.

i suckle on
your skin and
i can taste your
salty nectar in
endless abundance.

in the heat
of the moment
your silky skin
get inundated with
a brackish nectar.

in the heat
of the moment
even your briny flavours
taste sweet.

She Said…

she messaged him
saying…
loving you more today
than yesterday
and
i know you'll give me
another reason today
to love you more
tomorrow.

little did she know
she just gave him
another reason
to love her
even more.

r. A. bentinck

Slow and Easy

i wanna sync
with your every
motion.

i wanna take it
slow and easy
savouring every aspect
of your sexuality.

i wanna hear
each heartbeat,
each accelerated breath,
each satisfactory moan.

i wanna feel
each slippery surface,
each tight grip.

i wanna sync
with your every

Seduced

emotion.
i wanna take it
slow and easy
tasting every aspect
of your sexual magnificence.

r. A. bentinck

Suddenly

suddenly,
i felt
erected nipples
kissing
my naked back
and
i froze with
an abrupt erection.

suddenly,
she nibbled on
my earlobe
as if it were chocolate
and i understood
her endearing intentions.

her fingers
roamed the pasture of
my maleness
while her persuasive lips

Seduced

glide by erogenous zones
at a slow
and
calculated pace.

suddenly,
she spun me around
and
subdued me
with a deep
tranquilising kiss.

r. A. bentinck

Fantasies

may i
fulfil
the prescriptions
to your ailing desires?

may i
resuscitate
your dying fantasies?

mat i
breathing
new life
of excitement
into your reality?

What You Gonna Do?

she stared
deep into my
vulnerabilities then asks,

"what you going to do
with me?"

with a tremulous smile
i replied

"i have a list of a thousand things
am going to do to you!"

she blushed as she strolled
by me with
the wickedest of smiles
engulfing
her delectable face.

r. A. bentinck

Whatever

however you want it
i will give it to you.
whatever it takes
to please you
i will do it to you.

i see your desires
burning brightly in
your eyes,
so whatever it
take
to satiate
those lustful cravings
i will do it
for you.

i can feel the claws
of your yearnings
devouring my flesh
and

Seduced

i feel your breath
of desire
enflaming my skin.

whatever it takes
to quench your
blazing needs
i will do it
to you.
i can hear
your heartbeat
drumming
with excitement.
tonight,
i will make music
with you.

whatever it takes
to make you sing lustily
i will do it
with you.

r. A. bentinck

Misinterpretation

don't be fooled by my quiet
unassuming exterior
there is a sultry fire
blazing in the depths
of my sensual soul.

i have in my possession
the necessary intellectual and physical
instruments
to break your house down,
to increase
your screaming decibels,
to stimulate
your fluid flow,
and make you
weak in the knees.
i can nurture
the petals of your rose,
and activate
the curling of your toes.

Seduced

Don't Speak

shhhh…
don't speak.
we need no words
at this juncture.
you don't need to remind me
of your love i can feel it
in every beat of your heart.

shhhh…
don't say
another word
i can feel
your need for me
in your comforting
embrace.

shhhh…
don't speak
we need no words
at this moment.

r. A. bentinck

Your Embrace

you wrap me in
your comfy embrace
and
the lingering troubles
of my day slip
into oblivion.

you squeeze me
with your summery desires
and i can
feel your friendly fire.

you swaddle me
in caring arms
and i get lost
in your loving-kindness.

Seduced

One More Time

i don't know
why you did
what you did
to me but
do it to me
one more time.

i'm not sure
you know how
this makes me feel
so just do it
one more time.

you have
unshackle my
unaddressed yearnings
please,
give it
to me one more time.

Just to Please

i'm slow
and
deliberate,
just to please
you.

my attention
to details
are to guarantee
your total satisfaction.

the dexterity
of my
tender-hearted touches
are done with
one objective in mind,
i want
to please you
totally.

The Teasing Game

your flower piqued my curiosity
and triggered my quest
to study her intricate details.

each exploratory touch
revealed so much.

the stroking
of her stamen
yield a quivering
reaction accompanied
by a flood of fluid excitement
saturating the surface
of her petals.
your eyes locked
with mine
halfway through the exploration
and pleaded with me
to continue exploring.

r. A. bentinck

Unfulfilled Desires

it shows in your
expressive eyes
that speaks of insatiable thirst.

too long
in starvation,
trapped by wild
pesky desires.

you have become
skilled at masking
your chafe cravings.

pretend at your own peril.
how long do you want to hide
the way you feel within?
i have the remedy,
i have the serum
to unleash and satiate
your unfulfilled lust.

All Yours

turn on the red light
and tell me
your surreptitious secrets.

slide out of
your silk dress
and tell me
your deepest
darkest desires.

baby, it's all yours,
this is your
satisfaction sanctuary
and i'm here
to please.
may i give it to you
all through the night…
baby,
i'm all yours.

r. A. bentinck

Finally

finally,
after aeons of running around
in my pipedreams
we collide.

finally,
after all those
moments of make belief
sensual heat,
we get the privilege
to burn in
each other's flame.

finally,
i get the opportunity
to succumb to
the power of
your delicious allurements.
finally,
i savour the experience

Seduced

of all

your delectable flavours.

finally,

i can feel

the sweetness

of looking into

your sinless eyes.

r. A. bentinck

Those Moments

you know how
to manipulate
my breath,

you know how
to tease
the logical reasoning
out of me.

you know how
to drive me
insane
just enough to
keep me yearning
for more
and more
of you.

i sit here in
the company of those

Seduced

ephemeral memories
and the vivid pictures
still, rob me of
logical thinking,
and leave me senseless.

r. A. bentinck

Led

softly…
she held
my hands and
took me to
the sponge cloud
and lay me gently
for a heavenly ride.

skilfully…
she gradually
turned up
the heat,
bit by bit
by bit
till i lose all
my senses and control.

tenderly…
she guided me
through rocky roads,
aided me through

Seduced

bumps and grinds,
through all
the countless
ins and outs.

sweetly…
she kissed me back
to a relaxing
reality where
my heartbeat slowly
returned to normalcy.

r. A. bentinck

Roaming Tongue

aimlessly it seems
but
somehow she knows
how to find
those erogenous zones.

with skilled precision
and
subtle dexterity
she knows
how to please.

her controlled
and
varied pace
with just enough moisture
send a rush of
unexpected reactions:
toes curl,
fingers grab,

Seduced

nails claw,
and
high pitch sounds
enliven the atmosphere.

she has a
masters in pleasing.

r. A. bentinck

She is Unbelievable

she takes me
to places that
seem surreal.

she makes love feels
crazy,
freeing,
adventurous
and
memorable.

she knows how to
leave a lingering smile
on my face
and
countless wow complements
on the tips of
my satisfied tongue.

In the Rain

surprisingly it
approached with whipping
crystal missiles
exploding against
our parched skin,
everyone pelted for shelter
except for us.

she peered into my eyes
through the haze of
crystal pellets
and
the unspoken message
was clear,
we will continue strolling.
our fingers embraced,
while we disturb
puddles of water
making delightful splashes,
we skipped

r. A. bentinck

like carefree children
at play-
all in the pouring rain.

it was one of those
spontaneous moments
where unknowingly
we grew
closer and stronger,
the beauty of this
fugacious occasion
leave an indelible stain
we don't wish
to erase.

The Artist at Work

she asserted.
spread my legs
like your easel
and
paint me with
your sweetest phantasms.

she pleaded…
dip your brush
in my palette
and
mix my pigments
so my vivid colours
can burst on the
surface of
the naked canvas.

she implored!
baby, please
don't stop painting!
i adore

r. A. bentinck

the rhythm of
your brush-strokes
and
the painterly effect
it leaves on my soul.

Undressing

the sound of her
tight fitted jeans
unzipping
awoke
my carnal senses.

each…
zip,
zip,
zip,
zipping sound
massaged
my sensuosity.

her glacial and studied
unbuttoning of
the sleek blouse
further
enflamed my already
hyped-up appetencies.

r. A. bentinck

excited anticipation
embraced me as
i waited
uncomplainingly
for the conclusion.

Seduced

<u>Turning Petals</u>

i turned

the pages of her rose

and

slowly she began

to read me

her story.

line by line.

i strummed on

her sensitive cord

with my favourite finger

and

she started

singing

sweet songs

of appreciation

to me.

r. A. bentinck

Rhythms

your

slow parting lips,

your

rhythmic hips,

your

exploring hands,

your

gripping fingers,

your

panting breath,

your

low whispers,

your

gleeful pleas

your

exploding fluids

you are

a symphony of sensuality.

Waiting

deliberately,
i kept her waiting
and waiting.

repeatedly,
i took her to
the edge of ecstasy.

slowly,
i search to find
every erotic zone.

watchfully,
i observed her every move
manipulating the intensity
of each aroused desire.

deliberately,
i kept her waiting and waiting.
waiting for sweet release.

r. A. bentinck

Unfinished

we rolled
in
opposite directions…
panting,
gasping,
smiling,
laughing,
and caught in
the clutch of amazement.

we glanced
at each other
and i knew
we weren't finished.

gently you
took me and
led me to the place
where extreme ecstasy
flowed abundantly.

Seduced

Poetess

i slid between
your rhythms and rhymes
just to find the
right lines.

i frolicked
with your onomatopoeia
just to hear
your pleasure sounds.

i danced with
your similes
just to find
their similarities.

i stayed in
your moments just to
record your words.

r. A. bentinck

Satisfaction

too satisfied

to be bothered

we lay in

the laziness

of the moment

taking in the

sounds and feelings

of the sensual afterglow.

In the Dark

pitch black
but bright with desires,
i fumbled to find
her essence.

she held
my stiffness
and
guided me to the door of
her luscious sweetness.

i couldn't contain
the explosive excitement
that lit up the darkness.

r. A. bentinck

Glistening

she had that
glistening look,
her pores opened
and oiled her
with delight.

she has
that satisfied look
in her eyes and
a mile-wide smile
that spoke volumes.

she had that
glistening look
because
she was oiled
with
satisfaction.

Chasing Flavours

irresistible
was
the best way
to describe her.

one taste of
her essence
left me
wanting
more and more
and
more.

soon i was caught up
in the chase-
chasing
after her flavours.
chasing
after her irresistibility.

r. A. bentinck

Doing Dishes

the slow process
of
lathering
and
rinsing,

the slippery
ease with
which she squeezes
the foam,

the sensual arch
in her back
and
the periodic
twitch of her hips
leave me senseless
in a neutral corner
of the kitchen.

Her

touch her,
smell her,
love her,
tease her,
please her.

whisper to her words
she longed to hear.

hold her close
to the walls of your heart
and make her
feel safe.
mesmerise her,
leave her breathless,
leave her wanting,
leave her
with wild desires.
find ways to satisfy her.

r. A. bentinck

One

one look

one touch

one word

one kiss

one
    embrace.

one
    whisper

one

started

the journey

on this

unspeakable

experience.

all it took was

one.

Seduced

<u>Picking Fruits</u>

her tree is
laden…
all her fruits are ripe.

i picked
her cherries
and her leaves begin
to rustle,

i tasted
her mangoes
and her trunk begin to bend,

i suckle
on the juice
of her berries
and she begins
to shake
uncontrollably.

r. A. bentinck

<u>Secrets</u>

i kissed her lips
and
her secrets
began to unfold.

she had
enough
fire inside to burn
the village down,

she had
so much
softness
even rose petals
got jealous,

she had
tenderness
to last
and

Seduced

last and last.
she had
so much
frenzy
that
wild horses
seemed tamed.

r. A. bentinck

Tell Me

don't wait
say it to me
now.

tell me
your deepest thirst.

tell me
about those
unspeakable urges.

say it
to me
in simple words.

tell me how to
please you.
tell me what
tease you,
tell me.

You're

you're my reoccurring
fantasy.

you're that sweet
aftertaste
in my mouth
that increases
my yearnings.

you're the heat in my flames,

you're the slippery in my slide,
the joy
in my rides,
you're the bend in my bow.

you're the reason i smile
in places others can't see.

r. A. bentinck

The Proclamation

she proclaimed,

babe,
your tenderness
make me
extremely weak

and

your machismo
make me
wet and slippery.

Instigating

something about her
instigated the fling.

was it
the lure of her legs?
or was it
the tease in her tongue?

something
in her that
provoked this fling.

was it
her intellectual brilliance?
or was it
her inviting countenance?
everything about her
instigated a fling.

r. A. bentinck

Let Me

indulge me.

let me be

the flavours

you yearn for

when you get

those

irresistible cravings.

let me satisfy

your quenchless appetite.

encourage me.

let me be

the answers to

your complex questions

and

let me solve

your unsolved mysteries.

Dangerous

our eyes greeted
and i froze in
a moment of impaired attraction.

no words just that constant…
am undressing you
with my eyes
kind of gaze
and
when she finally spoke
it was her words
that stripped me.
made my knees
weak.
excited me.
teased me.

there is an inherent danger
in looking into
her eyes.

r. A. bentinck

Midnight

you are awake
in my mind
and prancing in style.

i'm grappling
with your pervasive
sexiness all over again.

it's midnight
and
i can't sleep,
there are too many
thoughts of you
battling to
seduce me.

Seduced

My Plea

i am trying baby,
but i am tired of fighting these
surging urges.

i can't conceal them anymore,
i don't want to fight any longer.

you set me afire,
you ignite the fuel in
the depths of my soul.

it's the effortless ease in which
you carry your natural blessings.
it's the electricity in your inviting eyes.
it's the trailing scent of your
hypnotising perfume.
it's your charming and
friendly personality.
it's your sensuous simplicity.
baby, please.

r. A. bentinck

i am counting my lucky stars and
consulting shamans
hoping that i have a fighting chance.

my wilting willpower has
grown weary,
and my reliable resistance is
getting weaker.

i'm tired baby,
have mercy on me.
baby,
please, i am weak.

Touched

i fondled
her mind
and
her body
erupted in ablaze.

i stimulated
her curiosity
and
a kaleidoscope
of emotions
overflowed.

i listened
to her yearnings
and
she rewarded me
with a bouquet of ecstasy.

r. A. bentinck

Transgressing Eyes

she perused
my body with fleshly intent,
taking in every conceivable inch
with starved eyes.

it felt like she was deliberately
undressing me
in public.

she had
a concupiscence look
in her eyes
with a lavish smile
that made me
twitchy.
i felt antsy
but adventurous
at the possibilities
of what she would
do to me.

In this Moment

in this moment
nothing else
will matter.

in that place
i promise to stay in the moment
with you.
taking in all of you,
feeling all of you,
appreciating
all you have to offer.

in this moment
the only thing
that matter is me
being here with you.

r. A. bentinck

Tonight

i can sleep
with ease
you have
filled me up with
sufficient goodness.

your legs straddle me
delicately,
and
your reassuring arms
remind me of
how much you care.

tonight,
i can fall asleep
with a peace filled mind
just because you are
here
next to me.

Of all the Things

of all the smiles
i have seen it's your smile
i want to continue
to brighten my life.

of all the things
i enjoy doing, it's doing you
i love the most.

of all the sounds
i enjoy hearing
it's your sounds
of gratification
i want to listen to
more and more.

of all the arms
that has held me
close it's your arms
i want to hold the most.

r. A. bentinck

Velvet Screams

muffled yet audible,
she buried her head
in the bosom
of the fluffy pillow
when she couldn't take
the intense pressures
of pleasure
anymore.

her velvet screams
was music
worth hearing.
they seeped through
the fibers of the pillow
while she contorts
with euphoria.

One Dance
(Gingerbay Café)

in a dimly lit café
her natural beauty
illuminated the table.

soft red light gently caresses
her luscious features
as slow reggae jams
dominate the cosy space.

Beres Hammond was
at his vintage best,
so i asked her for one dance.

that night,
the DJ was indulging in musical sorcery-
with every selection,
we sink
deeper
and

r. A. bentinck

deeper
and
deeper
in a sea of romantic fantasies.

her now warm body so soft
i can taste her silky smoothness,
her head upon my chest as the lyrics
take us away captives,
my lips refashioned
from whispering honeyed words,
to playfully pecking her forehead
to lightly caressing
her irresistible lips.

we are now drifting in musical waves
where slow dancehall
bump and grind
evoke fast and choppy breaths.
sensual rhythms tie us up so close
that the tip of my nose
skim across her steaming body
the heat…
radiates the soothing fragrance

Seduced

of her arresting perfume
i am anchored!

we are lost in this dancehall sea
and time no longer has meaning
as we sail on from one
musical selection to another,
riding the waves of a multitude of
lyrical passion.

r. A. bentinck

Falling Clothes

in the fervour
of the moment
her clothes
began to drop
like dried leaves
in the gentle wind.

they collapsed in
a crumpled heap
below her dainty feet.

she stood there
like an unfinished masterpiece,
waiting for the master sculptor
to apply
his finishing touches.

Seduced

Don't Make Me Wait

it's a slow
and
immeasurable tease.

she knows how much
i want her
but she keeps me
waiting,
and waiting, and
waiting.

the burgeoning
ache of anticipation
coupled with
my loaded imagination
leave my heart
in a spin.
my palm is
sweaty
and now i'm breathless.

r. A. bentinck

Fatal Whispers

her approach
was slow, sleek
and calculating.

she leaned over
with a devilish ease
and whispered
in the halls of my eager ears…

i'm the temptation
you are too weak to resist.

i'm the seductress
who will tame
your wildness.

i shuddered
from a mix of
momentary fear
and adventurous excitement.

Her Skirt

her skirt,
long enough to
conceal her tease
and
short enough to
explode the ticking
imagination.

her skirt,
tight enough to
caress each sensual curve
and
loose enough to
facilitate her
elegant strides.

r. A. bentinck

Scented Trail

she left a scented trail
of perfumed seduction
that could be traced
to the bedroom.

led by my now
uncontrollable
bloodhound yearnings
i tracked
her temptation.

she was reclining
effortlessly with
a mischievous smile
glazed on her cute
babyface.

Seduced

The Wild Side

take my hands
let me walk you
to the wild side.

hold me close
when your heart
begin to race
with excitement.

follow my lead
while we explore
those unspoken fantasies.

grip me tighter
when the action
get too racy
for you to take.
sync with me
while we ride

r. A. bentinck

through the torrid
patches of unending
desires.

hold my hands
while we walk
the wild side.

Dirty Desires

the first time
we met,
she looked me
squarely in the eyes
then whispered
fondly,
i got the good stuff
you need.
and
i know how to please.

with a befuddled smile
i muttered,
i hear you cutie.

she got cosier
then
she murmured,
i'm not gonna
lie to you,

r. A. bentinck

every time
i see you
i have
dirty thoughts
and…
every time
i think of you,
i have
dirty desires…

you know i'm
living alone right?
wouldn't you
come home with me?

Steamy

the echo of her
pleasurable moans
swiftly
fill the space of
the small room.

her screams of
gratification
bounces off the walls
with excitement.

the bearable heat
from her toned body
clouded the crystal
windowpane.
we are now drenched
in salty pearls
that drizzled down
our sweltering bodies.

r. A. bentinck

Unchained Desires

may i **take you to**
sensual places
you have never
visited before?

may i **guide you to**
the brink of erotic explosions
where your senses
get wild?

may i **tease the triggers**
that makes
your liquid excitement
overflow?
make i **unlock those**
imprisoned desires
setting you afire
while i watch you
slow burn?

Seduced

Risqué Roulette

alternating
feathery touches by
trigger happy fingertips
leave us tense
with anticipation.

dirty words aimed
at our wilting
self-control and
bridled emotions.

eyes locked in
an unflinching
stare down while
begging lips quiver
from the stress of
persisting desires.
who will be
the first to give in?
who will be the first to break?

r. A. bentinck

Pillow Fight

like puppies at play
we tussle with
each other and
the sheets get rumpled
in the intense battle.

armed with
fluffy pillows,
mouths full of
playful chatter,
and
childlike enthusiasm
we wage war on each other.

amidst the prolonged
fun and romp
battle cries morphed
into escalating yearnings,
bulges and bumps
begin to show,

Seduced

tired breath
now sound like the calls
of thirsty desires,
we took noticed
and
calmly we surrendered
to the power of these
new urges
and melted into each
others sweetness.

r. A. bentinck

On the Phone

the world now
revolve around
the sound of your voice and
a piece of technology.

i'm enthralled by
your soothing yet tantalising tone.

you tell me about
your longings
and how the time
seem to be crawl like a snail.
you tell me about
your specific needs and
adventurous wants.
my imagination takes flight
as i devise strategies
to satiate all
your risqué needs when
we get home.

Seduced

Waking Me Up

her legs straddled
me in a slow and
sensuous motion
and the electric touch
of her finger was enough to open
my eyes.

it's midnight
and her pesky needs
coaxed her into waking me up.

her purposeful hands
wended its way to my loin
and sleep vanished at
the hands of her
sultry touches.
she woke me up
because she had
some unsatisfied
needs for me to please.

r. A. bentinck

I Love

i love the smell
of your hair
as i slide my fingers
through it.

i love the feel
of your skin
when i kiss
your forehead.

i love the sensation
of lying in your lap
while we relax
the moments away.

i love the look
in your eyes
when your lips
greet mine in
a welcoming kiss.

Seduced

there is a lot
to love about you
but most of all
i love
the simple occasions
i share with you.

r. A. bentinck

On Those Days

on those days
when i hear
your pacifying voice
on the phone,
if only i could reach
through the technological
barrier and hold you
how different
our conversation would be?

on those days
when distance separates us,
if only i could cast a spell
and change miles
into inches
how different
the experience would be?
some days i just
yearn to be
closer to you.

Magical Fingers

they know how and where
to touch me,
your fingers
drive me
screaming crazy.
  you have magical fingers.

your fingers have
a mind of their own
they know
when
to tease me
and when
to please me.
  your fingers are magical.

r. A. bentinck

Speechless

somewhere between your
breath-taking temptations
and
blinding beauty
i lose my ability
to speak.

somewhere
between you penetrating
my aroused senses
and rendering me dumbfounded,
you leave me
speechless
and
breathless.

Lavish Longings

the pulsating temptations
was too cogent
to oppose.

the congested room
was too small
for our lavish longings.

but we both yielded,
relinquishing the will
to withhold and control
letting
our glutton lust
lead the way.

r. A. bentinck

Morning Ride

waking up with
a morning thirst
for your sweetness.
reaching over
you interrupted me…
my morning breath!
what morning breath?

i can't smell or taste it,
all i can taste is
your succulent
and delectable lips.
i love
your sounds of ecstasy
which drowns out
the calls of
morning birds
at joyful play.
what a way
to break the new day.

Seduced

Shower Exist

your freshly shaven legs
emerged from behind
water stained doors
and you call out softly…

baby, pass my towel, please.
beads of water droplets
decorated the raised pores
on your water-drenched body.

you tossed back
freshly washed hair
and your sensuality meter
shot up to steamy readings.
the appetising fragrance
of your bath soap
lights up all my senses
and
your irresistible smile
just drives me wild.

r. A. bentinck

Come Back Baby

i know you had to go
but my heartbeat
keep playing a tune
that calling,
calling
for you…

come back, baby.
i didn't get enough
of you,
i didn't get all the time
i needed with you,
come back, baby.

i know it was late
and we were encroaching
on danger time,
you had to leave
immediately.
but i'm still yearning

Seduced

for you,
i'm still craving
second chances
of the moments we created,
i'm still salivating
from the memories
you left me.

come back baby,
i didn't get
a satisfactory amount
of your sweetness,

i didn't get to savour
your delectable flavours.
baby,
please come back.

r. A. bentinck

Dreams

if my dreams
were real i would be holding
you softly
while we watch
the waves kiss
the thirsty shore.

if dreams were real
you would be lying
in my arms
while i stroke
your silky hair
and listen to your stories.
if these dreams
were reality
i would have been
consumed by
your sweet fragrance
while we watch
the stars play in the sky.

Seduced

Take Back

please, take back
all these steamy memories
and risqué dreams.

take back
the bouquet of fragrance
you left in the halls
of my nostrils.

take back these sultry pictures
you painted on
my fertile mind.

please take back
all your fond memories,
my heart is flooded
you are absent but
your memories are
always present.

r. A. bentinck

Show Me the Way

there is no shame in asking.
show me the way
to your pleasure centres
where wild emotions
run free and they are
no limitations.

take my fingers and
guide them
to those areas that
make you tremble
with excitement.

show me the way
to the places
where you conceal
your unspoken longings.
just show me the way
and i will follow.

Rainy Days

these are the days
when i find frivolous excuses
not to leave the comfort
of our bed.

these are the days
when i rummage for reasons
to snuggle a little closer
just to absorb
your body heat.

these are the days
when laziness becomes
my close companion and
getting out of bed becomes
a laborious chore.
these are the days
when holding you close
feels sweeter than sweet.

r. A. bentinck

Whispers

bend down low
and whisper to me
those things you plan to
do to me
and
with me
when we are
finally alone.

come a little closer
and whisper in my ear
all the horny secrets
you wish no one
to hear.

bend down low
and
whisper those
sultry words
that make

Seduced

my imagination
volatile.
bend down low
and
whisper to me
once more.

r. A. bentinck

Give Me a Reason

give me a reason
to sneak away from
work, so i can fulfil
your insatiable needs.

please give me a reason
to drive for miles
just to be in
your presence
soaking up your sun.

give me another reason
to spend a little
more time on the phone
just listening to
the luring in your voice.
just give me a reason
to find creative ways
pleasing and teasing you
to the pinnacle of your daring desires.

Seduced

All Over Me

i sit in silence
and your memories
begin to enfold me.

the feelings of
your soft kisses,
the roaming adventures
of your magnetic fingers,

the essence of
your warm embrace,
the sound of your alluring voice,
the smell of
your favourite perfume,
the angelic look
in your eyes
and your ever-present smile.
i sit in contemplation
and your memories are
all over me.

r. A. bentinck

Underneath the Sheets

she takes me to
fairytale destinations
whenever we are
underneath the sheets.

the warmth and comfort
of this fabric seclusion
is one of our favoured
places to be.

our imaginations are
set free whenever we are
underneath the sheets.

we relinquish the need
to be morally correct,
to worry about
the stresses of the day.
this is where we
make and break rules

Seduced

willy-nilly.
underneath the sheets
is where we come
to quench our fiery desires.

r. A. bentinck

Drizzled Honey

in preparation for
the sensual feast
i drizzled honey
all over her already
delicious body.

each drip
and
dribbled line
created
an enticing trail to
erogenous regions.

the slow pours
were both torture
and
temptation.

tantalising
and

Seduced

teasing.
satisfying
and
seductive.

i decorated her body
with
drizzled honey
just to heighten
the sweetness of
the moment.

r. A. bentinck

Reflection

i saw her reflection
in the mirror
from the deliberate
half-opened bedroom door.

the mirror smiled at
her nakedness
while she applied
sweet fragrance to
her delightful skin.

her mirror smiled.
the curtain danced,
and i was frozen in admiration
of her reflection in the mirror.

Seduced

Fooling Around - Scene 1

she interrupted
my late night studying
with piercing nipples
like the tip of arrows
against my naked back.

she whispered softly
in my ear,
hey baby

then proceeded to
nibble on my earlobe.

my manhood began
to rebel in its confinement,
my logical voice
reminded me,

*you have an important
exam tomorrow,*

r. A. bentinck

stay focus!
ugh!
i hate it my logical voice
is always correct.

glancing over my shoulder
i watched her walk away
with a slow and
deliberate tease.
damn… she is irresistibly gorgeous.

Seduced

Fooling Around - Scene 2

i watched her
prepare for work
and like a cat approaching
an unsuspecting rat
i pounced on her
with a gentle hug
and baby kissed
on her neck.

not now, i'm late for work baby!
she reminded me.

my intentions were crystal clear,
all the suggestive signs
were evident.
i toyed with her exposed
erogenous spots
while she fixes her makeup.
it was my day off
and

r. A. bentinck

my mischief meter was amped up.
come on sweetie, just
a little piece it won't take long,
please?

she wrestled my tenderness away.

no… you are going to
mess up my makeup
and
you know what happened
the last time?

Seduced

Fooling Around - Scene 3

she stood in the doorway
dangling a Chiquita banana
in my visual field.

glancing over her shoulder
at me with a tantalising stare
she proceeded to peel it
slow and suggestively.

she flicked her flowing locks
aside while she gently
bite down on the soft meat.

with a desiring gaze,
an impish smile
and
a mischievous tone
she asked quietly,
would you like a piece hon?

r. A. bentinck

P.M. Scenes

the sun is at its peak.
and
an urgent need to
please and appease
raging libidos surfaced.

our synchronising hormones
were at their optimum,
so we initiated a
well-planned getaway
to satiate our mutual needs.

now we are
sprawled out with satisfaction.

our dishevelled hair,
the wrinkled,
disorganise and
liquid stained sheets
tell the whole story.

Seduced

our skin glistened
from excess perspiration.

our languid bodies lay
stretched out in
a room filled with
the smell of satisfaction.

r. A. bentinck

Slow Surrender

it was never about
how but when.
the process was long
and tantalisingly excruciating.

her daily
drips of temptation.
her deliberate tease
and tauntings.

the excessive flaunting
of her natural assets.
my increasingly feeble
willpower eventually
wilted.

i surrendered to
the callings of
her natural tormentors.

Unbuttoning

my heart galloped
with anticipation.

the imagination is
riddled
with alluring imageries.

my loins ache
because of hyper contracting
muscles.

her unbuttoning
process
is slow and sleazy.
she is doing it
at this pace
just to torture
my will to wait.

r. A. bentinck

Pretty Feet

when her feet
hit the floor
even the boards
smile with appreciation.

her dainty toes
have a way of toying
with me.

she has pleasing feet.

i love to see
her bare feet
but they are even
lovelier in heels.
her feet appeal to me.

Seduced

Lustful Longing

as soon as i
opened the door
she arrested me!

pinned me
up against
the cold wall
and
unleashed her
raging desires
on me.

the buttons on
my brand-new shirt
flew like misguided missiles
everywhere.

r. A. bentinck

Don't Stop

oh, baby, please
don't stop now.

you've brought me
to a place
where i have never been
before and it feels
electrifying.

i'm feeling
feelings i've seldom felt before.

don't stop baby,
it feels real good.
even though
am breathless
and my face is contorted
with blissful agony
keep going.
don't stop!

Seduced

Penetration

it's the look in
your eyes
that pierces my core
making me want
you more.

it's the feeling i get
when you are near me
that question my ability
to please you.

it's the sound
of you soft breathe that
entice my imagination
and turns up the heat
in my emotional thermostat.
it's the unassuming
things about you that
penetrates me deeply.

r. A. bentinck

Let's Do It Again

what did you just do to me?
you have me
screaming my head off
in ecstasy.

you have
rearranged my senses,
you have
redefined my definition
of the expression,
'blow my mind'
and
you have me searching
for my next breath.

my squeals are
so loud that
we risk becoming
the neighbourhood noise nuisance.
i buried my head

Seduced

in the pillow
to muffle the loudness
but even the pillow
fails to contain
these uncontrollable sounds.

what did you just do to me?
let's do it again!

r. A. bentinck

Sleepless

a flooded mind,
and an overactive imagination
laced with a plethora of
her enticing imagery.

my sleep is at the mercy of
her bodacious memories.

tired eyes,
an overactive mind,
nodding head,
but i wouldn't go to bed.

i want her now,
i want her
before i go to sleep.

Seduced

<u>Nightly Pleasures</u>

sweet seducing sounds
caressing my eardrum.

she is making music
with me.

stealthily,
her fingers glide across
miles of desires.

sexily,
she whispers words
that causes spontaneous eruptions
inside of me.
my baby knows how to
tease and please me.

r. A. bentinck

I Need More

leave your door unlocked,
turn off the lights and
light the scented candles.

pour two glasses
of your favourite wine.

i'm coming over for
more
and more
and more…
more of what you gave me
last night.

more of what left me
breathless and in a love stupor.
more of what cause me to be
wanting more
and more
and more

Seduced

of you.
baby,
i am planning to make up
all the lost hours.

i need more
and more
and more
more of what you give me
last night.

give me all of you,
i need more,
and more
and more,
more of what you
gave me last night.

r. A. bentinck

The Spot

after endless searches
he finally found
her arduous pleasure spot.

her eyes
glowed with delight,
her body buckles under
the pressure of excess pleasure

and

she whispered
sweetly
with a trembling voice,
don't stop baby,
please, don't stop.

Seduced

The Text Message

last night was magical!
your fingers were electric
and your tongue
was ineffable.

it seems like every part
of me you touched
just heightened
the pleasure experiences.

i love your creativity
in the kitchen,
your explosiveness
in the bedroom
and your tenderness in
the bathroom.
ooh, baby,
it still turns me on
just thinking about it.

r. A. bentinck

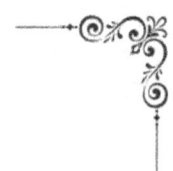

Scream My Name

i must be doing
something right,
we are both
sweaty and slippery
and you are
screaming out
my name,
pleading with me for
more and more
of the same.

breathe baby, breathe.

i must be doing
something very right,
we are both
fiending for more
and more of this breath-taking
experience.

Seduced

Flavours

i have tasted you.
now,
your irresistible flavours
are tattooed to my taste buds.

i have tasted those
gratifying flavours,
which are impossible
to forget.

they are plastered on
the decorated walls of
my prolific memory
and
they arbitrarily set
my body afire.

r. A. bentinck

Intimidation

she sized me up
from across the room.

she approached me
with confident strides,
stare me
dead in the eyes
then said bluntly,

i will do things
to you
and
with you
that you will
never ever forget.

Burn Baby

here it is,
the precise moment
you have worked
diligently for.

the time is right,
this generous mood is idle.
ignite me.

poke your polished wood in
my unquenchable fire,
make me
burn.
burn,
baby,
burn.
watch me eagerly
while i blaze fiercely
out of control.
heed my passionate pleas

r. A. bentinck

for more of
your fiery heat.
faithfully attend to my sparks
while they constantly fly
and
add earnestly more wood
to my smouldering fire.

make me
burn.
burn,
baby, burn.

Exploration

i lose myself
and find myself
with you.

tonight,
we will carefully explore
all the available options.

let's willingly unchain
our bridled passion,

let's
gently give in to
our feral desires,
let's intentionally lose
our restrained self-control
and go with
the spontaneous flow.

r. A. bentinck

Catch the Fire

you carefully lit me up
like a solitary candle
in the dark.

you politely ask for
more dazzling light
and burn brighter.

you ask for
more heat
and my fierce flames
got hotter.

my wax melted rapidly
and i started
to worry about
my ability
to sustain
the consuming fire
you crave.

Gradually

it was more
a slow burn
than
an engulfing flame.

her essence
and
her charm
took hold of me
s l o w l y.

she squeezed her way
into my daily thoughts
and
dominated my dreams.

r. A. bentinck

I Can't Explain

one look at her
and suddenly my blood
start racing
through my veins
then i lose self-control.

time after time
i try gallantly to figure out
what she has over me.

when thoughts of her
dominate my mind
my heartbeat multiply times five.
i can't explain what
she has over me.
the thought and sight
of her make me weak.
my fierce resistance
rapidly fade at the mention
of her name.

The Phone Call

ring, ring, ring,
her: hey hon, how are you?

him: i'm fine and how
are you beautiful?

her: i could be better
if you were over here
and tear up all of
this goodness.

him: ha, ha, ha.

her: am very serious,
you need to be here baby,
i'm craving all of you.
him: give me a few minutes
i'll be there in a jiffy,
click.

r. A. bentinck

The Taste of You

i have tasted you
now,
your irresistible flavours
are tattooed all over
my taste buds.

i have tasted
those gratifying flavours,
now they are
impossible to forget.

they are painted on
the walls of
my prolific memory
and
they randomly set
my body ablaze.

Thirst

you poured
the opulence
of your essence
on my parched desires.

you opened
the floodgates
to my
starving lust
and
quenched
my
passionate longing
for sweet relief.

r. A. bentinck

Forbidden

just because
they said
it shouldn't be done
we did it with gusto!

they said it was
too early to feel
this passionately
about each other
but we felt it anyway.

just because
it produced so much
exhilarating fun
we continue to
do it with pizzazz.

The Kitchen Counter

this is where
the meat and fish
get chopped and seasoned.

this is where
the finer details
of the meal
get planned and prepared.

this is the heart
of the cooking activities.
but today,
the experience is different.

this is where
the love escapade is
laid out
and
played out.
this is where

r. A. bentinck

bodies get tossed and turned.
this is where
the bone merges
with the meat.

this is where
the seasoning is
in the thinking
and the cooking is
in the doing.
this is where
no salt is needed
to add flavour.

this is where
no sugar is added
to make it sweeter.

this is where
no pepper is needed
to make it hot.
just bodies
obeying the laws
of sensorial gratification.

Climaxing

a slow
and
spine teasing
build-up.

a soft
and
sensual touch
transposed into
passionate
and hair-raising
grabbing.

butterfly kisses
morph into steamy
tongue wrestling,
while our heartbeat
gallops like racehorses
frolicking in the fields.

r. A. bentinck

About The Author

r. A. bentinck has several published books. He was very active in the theatre scene in Guyana during the 90s where he acted in many major productions at the Theatre Guild of Guyana and the National Cultural Centre.

As a visual artist, he has been a part of several national exhibitions, and his work represented Guyana at Carifesta IX, held in Trinidad and Tobago in 2006.

Seduced

He has been very active in sports and youth development. He was the chaperone for a youth contingent from Guyana for the first Habitat for Humanity Caribbean Youth Build held in 2000.

'Of all the Lilies' is Bentinck's debut poetry collection published in 2017. This collection features a rich array of poems and prose about various life experiences.

Bentinck is originally from the county of Berbice in Guyana but spent most of his adult life in the capital Georgetown.

www.ingramcontent.com/pod-product-compliance
Lightning Source LLC
Chambersburg PA
CBHW031639040426
42453CB00006B/155